OJIBWA

ABORIGINAL
PEOPLES OF
CANADA

Michelle Lomberg

Published by Weigl Educational Publishers Limited
6325 10 Street S.E.
Calgary, Alberta, Canada
T2H 2Z9

Website: www.weigl.com
Copyright ©2010 Weigl Educational Publishers Limited

Library and Archives Canada Cataloguing in Publication data available upon request.
Fax 403-233-7769 for the attention of the Publishing Records department.

ISBN 978-1-55388-998-4 (hard cover)
ISBN 978-1-55388-511-5 (soft cover)

Printed in the United States of America
1 2 3 4 5 6 7 8 9 13 12 11 10 09

Photograph and Text Credits

Cover: Canadian Museum of Civilization (III-G-883 a, b); Alamy: pages 4, 7; Canadian Museum of Civilization: pages 9T (V-F-6, D2004-27013), 9M (III-G-883 a, b), 9B (V-F-135 a, b), 12B (III-G-178, D2003-07523), 15B (III-G-364 a,b, D2003-07523), 17B (III-G-728, D2004-228343), 20 (III-G-711 a-b, D2004-22148), 21 (III-G-514, D2004-22306), 23 (III-G-503, D2003-10272); Corbis: pages 1, 6, 10L, 13, 14, 16, 17T; CP Images: page 8; Getty Images: pages 5, 10M, 10R, 11L, 11M, 11R, 12T, 15T

Every reasonable effort has been made to trace ownership and to obtain permission to reprint copyright material. The publishers would be
pleased to have any errors or omissions brought to their attention so that they may be corrected in subsequent printings.

All of the Internet URLs given in the book were valid at the time of publication. However, due to the dynamic nature of the Internet, some
addresses may have changed, or sites may have ceased to exist since publication. While the author and publisher regret any inconvenience
this may cause readers, no responsibility for any such changes can be accepted by either the author or the publisher.

We gratefully acknowledge the financial support of the Government of Canada through the Book Publishing Industry Development
Program (BPIDP) for our publishing activities.

PROJECT COORDINATOR Heather Kissock

DESIGN Terry Paulhus, Kenzie Browne

ILLUSTRATOR Martha Jablonski-Jones

Contents

The People

The Ojibwa are a **First Nation**. Their **traditional** lands covered the present-day provinces of Saskatchewan, Manitoba, and Ontario in Canada, as well as North Dakota, Minnesota, Wisconsin, and Michigan in the United States.

There are three Ojibwa groups. The Plains Ojibwa lived on the prairies of Manitoba, Saskatchewan, and North Dakota. The Woodlands Ojibwa lived in the forests of Michigan, Minnesota, Wisconsin, and south-central Ontario. The Northern Ojibwa lived in the forests of northern Manitoba and Ontario.

NET LINK

To find out the meaning of Ojibwa, go to **www.everyculture.com/North-America/ Ojibwa-Orientation.html**.

Ojibwa Homes

WIGWAM In the past, the Ojibwa lived in wigwams. A wigwam was a dome-shaped house. It was made of wood, **rush mats**, and birchbark. Wooden poles were bent to make the house's frame. The rush mats and birchbark were then laid over the frame to make walls.

Ojibwa Ideas

Birchbark is water resistant. This means it takes a long time for water to soak through it. The Ojibwa used birchbark to build their wigwams because it kept the inside dry.

A fire was built in the centre of the wigwam. It provided heat and light. People sat and slept on mats and furs that were spread across the wigwam's floor.

Ojibwa Clothing

DRESSES AND LEGGINGS

Women wore dresses and leggings. These clothes were made from animal hide.

SHIRTS AND LEGGINGS

Men wore shirts and leggings. Like women's clothing, these clothes were made from animal hide.

DECORATION

The Ojibwa often decorated their clothing with porcupine quills. The quills were dyed to be different colours. Plants were used to make the dye.

ROBES AND MITTENS

When the weather became cold, the Ojibwa wore robes and mittens made from animal fur.

MOCCASINS

The Ojibwa wore moccasins to protect their feet. These shoes were made from animal hide.

Hunting and Gathering

WILD RICE

Wild rice grows in shallow water. The Ojibwa dried and boiled wild rice. They then ate it with meat or fowl.

BERRIES

The Ojibwa picked chokecherries and raspberries. The berries were dried, eaten fresh, or made into a paste.

BISON

Bison meat was often made into pemmican. This is a mixture of meat, fat, and berries. Pemmican was dried and stored for later use.

In the past, the Ojibwa found food in nature. As each Ojibwa group lived in a different area, their foods varied. The Plains Ojibwa relied on bison. The Northern Ojibwa hunted deer and moose. The Woodlands Ojibwa used sap from maple trees.

TREE SAP
The sap from maple trees was made into sugar and syrup. These could be used to sweeten other foods.

DRINKS
Wintergreen and spruce needles were used to add flavour to hot and cold drinks.

FISH
When near water, the Ojibwa fished for food. Trout, pickerel, and sturgeon were some of the fish they caught.

Ojibwa Tools

HUNTING AND FISHING

The Ojibwa made tools from materials found in nature. Fishing hooks were often carved from bone. Fish were pulled into a canoe using wooden fishing reels. Wood and stone were used to make bows and arrows. These were used to hunt land animals.

Ojibwa Ideas

When sewing clothing, the Ojibwa used animal sinew for thread. Sinew is what holds muscles to bones.

MAKING CLOTHING Sharpened bones were used to scrape and clean animal hides. **Awls** and needles made from bone and wood were used to sew clothing.

Moving from Place to Place

CANOES

In the past, the Ojibwa travelled by water or by land. They used birchbark to build canoes for water travel. The canoes were strong enough to use on fast-flowing rivers, but light enough to carry between rivers and lakes.

SNOWSHOES

In the winter, the Ojibwa used snowshoes to walk over the snowy land. The snowshoe frames were made of wood. Strips of animal hide were woven around the frames. Snowshoes are still used today, but less often than in the past.

NET LINK

To see how the Ojibwa built canoes, go to **www.native-art-in-canada.com/birchbarkcanoe.html**.

Ojibwa Music and Dance

Songs played an important role in Ojibwa life. Some songs were sung to entertain children and adults. Other songs helped people prepare for battle. A drum was often beat during the singing.

The Ojibwa used drums to play music and as a way to spread news. A drum would sound to announce the birth of a child, a marriage, or the end of a person's life.

Drums were played when the Ojibwa danced. Dancing took place at celebrations called powwows. These celebrations still take place today.

The Messenger of Spring

The Ojibwa have many stories to explain events that happen in the world. The story of a spirit called New Dawn describes how winter turns into spring.

In a world covered with snow and ice, New Dawn brings colour and life to Earth. Snow melts around him, and grass grows at his feet.

As the world begins to change, New Dawn meets Iceman, a spirit who once ruled over Earth. Iceman has grown old and tired, and is ready to leave the world he created.

New Dawn, on the other hand, is full of life. He sings a powerful song that warms the Sun, brings animals out of hiding, and makes the trees and flowers bloom.

As Iceman fades away, he leaves behind the gift of a flower. This special flower, called Spring Beauty, is a yearly sign that winter has faded and the new dawn of spring has taken its place.

Ojibwa Art

Art was part of daily life for the Ojibwa. Even items they used every day were always finely crafted. Baskets were made by weaving strips of bark together. Bowls, spoons, and other items were carved out of wood. These pieces were often decorated with **engraved** figures.

Ojibwa Ideas

When weaving baskets, the Ojibwa used different shades of bark to create patterns.

The Ojibwa used birchbark to create art. They would scratch a design into a folded piece of birchbark and then use their teeth to trace the design. When the bark was unfolded, the tooth marks left a delicate pattern in the bark.

Birchbark Biting with Wax Paper

Ingredients
Wax paper
Scissors

1. Cut a square of wax paper about 10 centimetres by 10 centimetres.
2. Fold the wax paper in half diagonally, making a triangle.
3. Fold the triangle in half along the center line, making a smaller triangle.
4. With your fingernail, scratch a design onto the wax paper triangle. Traditional Ojibwa designs include animals, birds, flowers, insects, and leaves. You can create your own design.
5. Use your teeth to bite into the wax paper, following along the design you traced with your fingernail. You do not have to bite through the wax paper. Just bite hard enough to leave a mark.
6. Unfold the wax paper to see the design you have made.

Glossary

awls: pointed tools used to make holes in animal hides

engraved: carved a design into wood or bone

First Nation: a member of Canada's Aboriginal community who is not Inuit or Métis

rush mats: floor coverings made from branches and bull rush

traditional: relating to beliefs, practices, and objects that have been passed down from one generation to the next

Index